Simply Words

MARGE FLORES

WESTBOW
PRESS®
A DIVISION OF THOMAS NELSON
& ZONDERVAN

WestBow Press books may be ordered through booksellers or by contacting:

WestBow Press
A Division of Thomas Nelson & Zondervan
1663 Liberty Drive
Bloomington, IN 47403
www.westbowpress.com
844-714-3454

ISBN: 979-8-3850-0157-6 (sc)
ISBN: 979-8-3850-0158-3 (e)

Library of Congress Control Number: 2023911922

Print information available on the last page.

WestBow Press rev. date: 07/26/2023

Dedication

To my husband Richard Flores, family Keino and Lucia Robinson, Matt Cote, Rich Flores, Corina Robinson, and Rich Robins. You have given my work a voice. Thank you my grand daughter for your artistic view of my work. And to my grandchild that said "I can do that for you." (Tech support). My book was complete.

Family is a gift that is given to an individual. Reality proves not all of us are fortunate in this area of life. So with a grateful heart I thank my family for their support in every detail of my book.

Acknowledgements

Rich Robbins - QR Codes
Van Rose - Illustrations
Goose Jelly - Technical Support
Family - Voices

Contents

Life has tried time and time again to extract payment
 from me,
Counting the cost for living.
But my value is mine,
Hard earned by the knocks of life.
Fought with determination to be true to myself.
Knocked down but never knocked out.
I will take time to inhale life as it is for me.
Inhale slowly, just to exhale deliberately,
And feel life's breath cleansing release.
With my senses alive, I determine what makes me, me.
My value will be drawn according to my palette of colors.
Rich vibrant transparency will be seen in my footsteps.
A life that was lived.

When I am told, "You can't,"
That's when I can.
When I feel that urge to explore,
I stretch myself into the possibilities,
Looking at my abilities to create.
For I am unique unto myself,
Exploring unfamiliar territory.

Ode to Friendship

It was as if I had known you forever
From the first time we met.
Nothing hidden from the other's heart,
Your hurt was mine, and mine was yours.
Battles were fought to the enemy's defeat.
We giggled as if little girls caught in the moment.
Laughed so hard our stomachs ached.
Forever till the end, you will be my best friend.

When I ask myself where the time went,
I look at my family, and I feel proud.
When I ask myself, "Why the aches and pains?"
I look over the years of work and toil.
I have loved my family through the years.
I know in my heart memories do not fail.
When loneliness crouches upon me,
I will reach for paper and pen and write.
When a tear runs down my cheek,
I will recognize I am blessed.

My mind is racing with thoughts, words, sentences.
My fingers move over the keyboard,
Blessed with autocorrect, at times.
It is like a song of words flowing onto the page,
Capturing the heartbeats of my poem.
I write in determination to my own deadline.
The dance I am in keeps tempo with me as I write,
A motion that projects me effortlessly forward.

Open Yourself

Open yourself to your worth.
You are much more than the sum of the outside world.
See where your yellow brick road leads.
Lay down your footprints to be followed.
Experience that which makes you unique.
You were never meant to fill a mold.

The one nobody notices.
The one who's not heard.
The one never picked for a team.
The one who stands and observes.

My heart sees you.
I hear your silence.
I see you as you stand alone.
I noticed you wear no team emblem.

I would be honored to have you as a teammate
For your quirkiness, silent strength, and quiet observation.
Intrigued by your potential against the competition.
You are proof that you are not an equal
But their rival.

Thoughts are like vapor; they have no power
Unless captured on paper, forever giving life.
A positive thought's breath can dissipate the negative
  thought.
A single directive could suffice in ending a thought.
Your mind is meant to create.
Capture that thought, and start forming it gently.
Let it evolve on its own to a point of beauty.
Remember to hold tight
To those otherwise fleeting thoughts.

Hearing

It is said hearing is the last sense to go.
Imagine lying in a hospital bed, last breaths coming,
Hearing your loved ones crying and begging you to fight,
Or while saying their goodbyes.
In hospice, lying there on your bed, and a sensitive
    nurse, aide, or worker
Telling you are not alone while holding your hand.
In your own bedroom, with family surrounding you,
Whispering how much you are loved,
Grateful for your part in their lives.

But what happens to the addict, someone suicidal,
A person facing drawn guns?
Who is there with reassurance that they are loved, will
    be missed,
The family left behind taken care of?
Are there no whispers of love, grateful words said of a
    life lived
Having touched someone in a positive way?

No whispers of, "Thank you for being in my life."
"Thank you for your love."

In a world of uncertainty, what last words will be heard?

It isn't necessary for you to point out my flaws.
You don't have to ask why I haven't …
Or stare at the obvious imperfections.
I'm well aware of your need to fix me.
I understand you can't ignore apparent evidence.
If I hold up a mirror, will you understand?
Correcting me isn't going to fix you.

The heart has no age.
Thoughts are formed by desires,
By experience flavored with curiosity.
You live forward, believing in life,
Looking for clues, answers, remedies to life.
What goes unnoticed is time.

In the moments of celebration,
May you always have family standing by you.
In the moments of heartache,
May they be there, holding you up.
In the moments of laughter,
May they enjoy the merriment.
In the moments of disbelief,
May they see the absurdity.
In the moments of achievement,
May they know the cost to you.
In the moments of brokenness,
May their arms hold you through defeat.
May you always have family standing by you
In the moment.

Supportive Hero, My Hero

There is a man in my life who is my support,
Someone I run to when I'm not sure.
I ask questions that may have obvious answers,
But he understands when I don't get it.
With tact he explains, which is a testament of his
  patience.

But when I am in my creative zone,
He will turn his world upside down to cover me.
He takes my responsibilities and makes them his own.
He sees and recognizes I am in a creative zone.
May not understand at first where I am going.
He doesn't need to see the path I'm on;
He has witnessed my potential.

I Sit and Wait

I sit and wait on you in quiet patience,
Amusing myself with life as it passes me by.
Knowing the wait is well worth any price.
I see a vision of love make its entrance.
Oh, the joy of knowing you are mine!
I smile in anticipation.
From the first time I saw you, I knew
I would never tire of your loveliness.

Paint Your Family Portrait

Your family portrait is unknown to you
Till the brush dipped in life touches the canvas.
Pour your family out on canvas.
Watch the colors so pure, so vibrant, mesh so well.
Yet distinctive in their own beauty,
Interlocking with warmth,
Bold in their identifying uniqueness,
Supporting while touching each other.
Watch their creativeness meet.
At times blending,
At times distinctly drawing borders.
This is your family's artistic poetry.
Your family portrait is unknown to you
Till the brush dipped in life touches the canvas.

Do you see?
Not with eyes but with heart.
I know you hear, but do you listen?
Are you capable of understanding me?
Don't prepare an answer for that was not the question.
Take a moment to remember,
To feel what you felt in that moment,
That moment when I matter.
Help me through this life
For what is the cost of an embrace?
A kiss in time to soothe an ache?
Dressed in loneliness, I go unnoticed.

Something about Me

When I share with you something I wrote,
And you start to read it but put it down
To never finish reading what I wrote,
It stings.
When I start to talk to you, to share a thought,
And see that light go out in your eyes,
It's smothering.
How aware are you of the moment?
When I come to you with my smile,
Begin to talk of something I believe is worth sharing,
Did you notice how straight your back gets?
Your chin slightly moves up; is that purposeful?
You see the moment is about me.
I wanted to share a story I wrote.
I wanted to share a moment.
Thoughts rummaging through my mind.
I come to you with a smile.
Your disdain is a neon sign.
I begin shutting down one piece at a time.

We were so young and did not know what the world
 held for us.
We only knew we wanted each other.
There were no plans of a future considered.
No savings, no insight, no thoughts of tomorrow.
But then two became three.
Reality was so painful.
This little one, looking at us with open expectancy of
 a bright future.
Where do we begin?

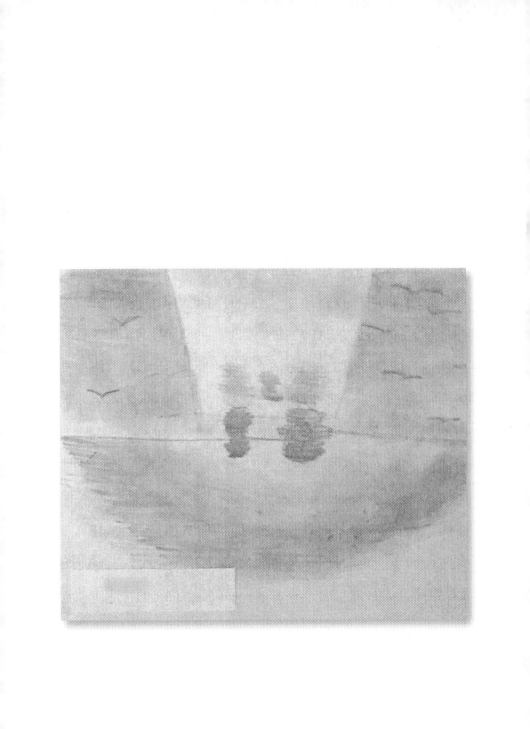

Are You Noticed?

As you sit there among us, do any of us talk with you?

As you eat a meal with us, do we offer to share?

As you stand within our circle, are we aware of you?

As you ride with us, do we make you part of the conversation?

As you see others get teased, are you teased with the same sense of love?

As you sleep in the same home, does someone kiss you good night?

Are you lonely in your family?

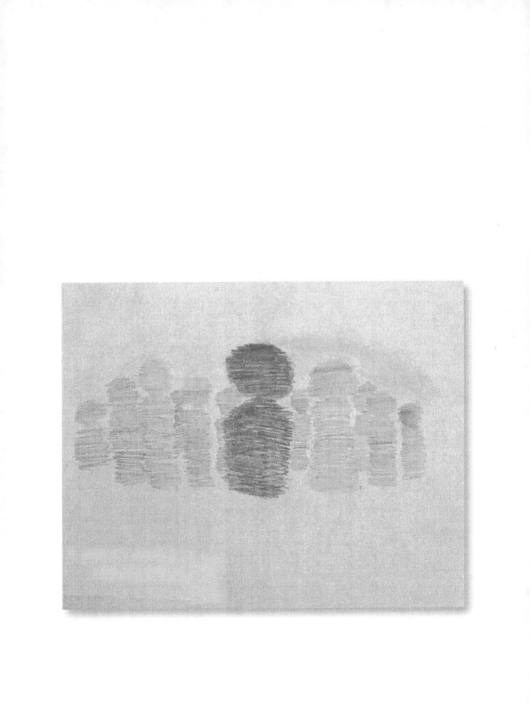

How important are you to you?

Do you truly know your self-worth?

Are there gaps, holes, disconnections?

Do you focus more on your failures than your accomplishments?

We all do some form of justifying who we are not and why.

Take time to unemotionally see your pluses and minuses.

Take one step at a time to build yourself up.

Build on your pluses, and turn your minuses around.

Grow slowly, and be specific about your individualism,

Not allowing others to define you.

Acceptance of who you are comes with knowledge.

No one can truly love you until you love yourself.

Age is not a factor; it's just a measurement of time.
Life is short, so keep your essence alive.
Allow your mistakes; use them as learning tools.
Grow within your heart, spirit, mind.
Be strong within yourself for yourself.
Age is but a measure of time.

At What Cost?

I was once asked by someone very close to me,
"Am I insensitive and overbearing?"
I wish I had enough courage to respond
In truthfulness, with love and respect.
Would that have made a difference?
Would she have considered my words,
Understood them as encouragement and made a change?
Could life have been sweeter?
I'll never know because I froze.
I did not want to speak the truth.
Didn't want on my heart that stain of hurt.
So I lived with her self-righteousness
And regretted that decision.

I enjoy freely opening my mind, then writing what
    I see.
It's like Scrabble tiles with words written on them,
Completing a whole sentence laid out before me.
Some make me laugh at the audacity of the thought,
While others bring a tear at the image that appears.
Writing frees me to discover a true me,
To enjoy thoughts that come to an open mind.

Stupid Anger

Anger by itself isn't wise.
It's an emotion drawn out by hurt feelings,
Uncontrollable in any circumstances.
Creates a need to defend oneself,
Tries one's patience to a tipping point.
But stupid anger is on one level—a stupid level.
This destructive emotion does not set one free.
Hurtful words are not the truth.
It sets people apart, isolating one from others.
It turns into a desire to be right—no matter the cost.
There is no righteousness to stupid anger.
No justification.
No victory achieved.
No happy ending.
Just collateral damage.

I See You

I know you are hurting; I see you.
I know you are frustrated; I sense it.
I know you are tired of waiting; I understand.
I know your anger isn't the cause of what I have done.
I know your silence is not meant to push me away.
I see you though, my love.

When your eyes looked into mine, was there a
connection?
Did the hug reveal a message to be understood?
Will a kiss reveal all that love promises to be?
May truth be the love that you have for me.
I want to wait for that love that can survive,
That takes me through all of time.
For love and my heart are one and the same.

There are some who walk into a kitchen,
And the atmosphere charges them.
Others sit at a piano, and the keys seem to play
themselves.
Inventors have ideas wrapped in desire.
A sculptor doesn't see a block of marble or a mound of
clay;
Rather, they are their next pieces of art.
Writers start with a blank page.
Painters work with paint, markers, pens, or charcoal
and a solid surface.
Talent and desire are driving forces behind their skills.
This feeds their souls.
Their struggles are very real; their feelings are seen in
their pieces.
It's done through their sweat, tears, and failures.
Art, in its many forms, is humanity.

Beauty of the Behold Her

Your beauty defined the moment I saw your face.
My heart was touched by your simple poise.
The softness of you never felt before.
Everything in miniature, perfectly portioned.
Newness in a simple form.
Eyes not yet opened; hands still clenched.
I smell your newness and ask myself,
"How can this be?"

Together Forever

I want to live our greatest moments while we are alive,
And let them be buried in the hearts of those who
survive.
There's nothing like looking at your spouse through the
lens of love,
Where the warmth of tenderness is alive.
Recounting moments as they are remembered,
Made all the sweeter by the witness of young minds.

I'm a cauldron of feelings
At the boiling point.
Words tumbling over each other, wanting out,
Desperately seeking their freedom of escape.
As popping out of a boiling kettle,
They do not hesitate.
Recklessly splattering letters everywhere
In that need to be liberated,
Leaving a mark forever.
Solid memory of "I was here."

Crossroads

When you find yourself at crossroads,
Be true to yourself, asking
What you can live through,
Knowing what you can live with,
Accepting what you can live without.
The path chosen should be your choice,
So on the other side of those tough times,
You know you were true to yourself.
It was your decision.
It wasn't made for you.